Amazing Auroras

Written by Mike Gould

Contents

Collins

T0321640

A very old painting

In 1885, a Danish teacher and amateur photographer called Sophus Tromholt published a book all about a weird natural phenomenon.

He had photographed some strange curtain-like lights in the sky while on his travels.

Unfortunately, he was unable to develop the photo so he drew what he remembered, then photographed his drawing for the book.

It is one of the first reliable pieces of evidence of an incredible natural wonder.

These lights – and similar ones near the South Pole – have cropped up in many stories, films, myths and legends.

This book is about how they are formed, and why they are so fascinating. It explains how they are created by a mighty clash between the forces of the Sun and Earth, and why people fear and worship them.

It explores why they are so much more than weird lights in the sky.

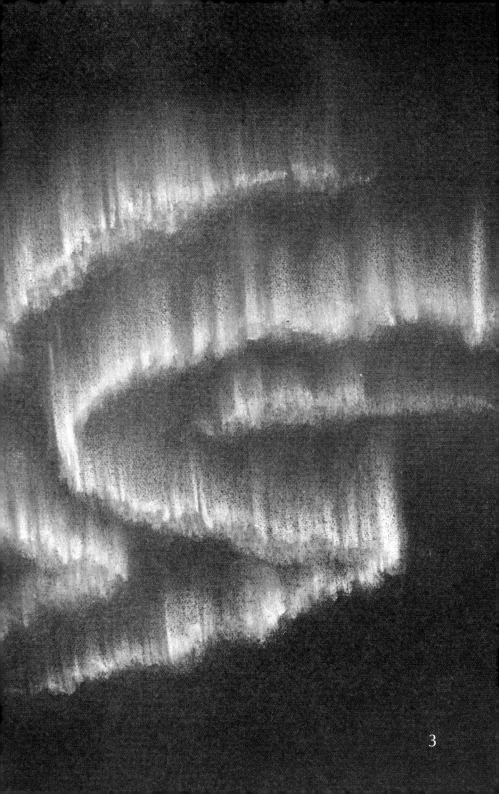

3

The amazing auroras

It was the Italian astronomer Galileo Galilei (1564–1642) who gave the lights you can see in the far north the name "aurora borealis" in 1619.

The word "aurora" comes from the name of the Roman goddess of the dawn. She travelled from east to west and announced the coming of the Sun. "Borealis" comes from the Greek name for the north wind.

If you are lucky, you can travel to see these lights today. They have been described as looking like rippling curtains or shooting rays. Sometimes, they form arcs or look like enormous ribbons hanging from the sky.

But where can you see them?

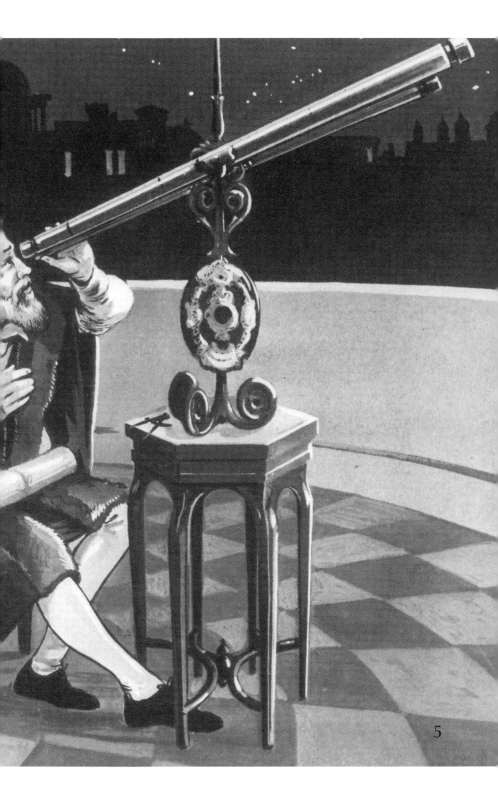

The aurora borealis are best seen in countries or places close to the Arctic circle (the area of Earth around the North Pole), such as Norway, Alaska and Siberia (a part of Russia).

The lights also appear in the southern **hemisphere** in countries such as Australia, Chile and Argentina nearer the South Pole. Here they are called "aurora australis". The word "australis" comes from the **Latin** word for "south land", and is also where the country Australia gets its name. So, these are the "southern lights".

When the lights appear in the southern hemisphere, they usually appear at the same time in the north.

northern hemisphere

southern hemisphere

How are the auroras formed?

Galileo was one of the first scientists to realise that Earth travelled around the Sun. But he believed the lights he saw were due to sunlight reflecting off the atmosphere. This wasn't quite right.

corona

In 1902–03, the Norwegian scientist Kristian Birkeland worked out exactly how the lights were formed.

He discovered it was all to do with something called the **solar** wind.

This "wind" is really just a flow of incredibly hot energy (around 10,000 degrees Celsius!), which emerges from the corona – the crown-shaped curve of the Sun's atmosphere. It carries an **electric charge** mostly made up of tiny **particles** called **electrons** and **protons**.

These electrically-charged particles shoot out towards Earth as part of the solar wind.

electrons

protons

The Earth is protected from solar winds by something called the "magnetosphere". The magnetosphere is the region of space where Earth's **magnetic field** is more powerful than the magnetic field of other planets. This is the same magnetism that makes a compass point to the symbol saying "N" for north when you hold it.

The magnetic field exists because of the electrical currents which flow from metals in Earth's outer core.

solar wind

solar wind

The magnetosphere is an important safety barrier for Earth. Without it, the solar wind would break through and much of life on Earth would be destroyed.

Inside the magnetosphere, the solar wind particles smash into Earth's atmosphere.

This is the battleground which creates the auroras.

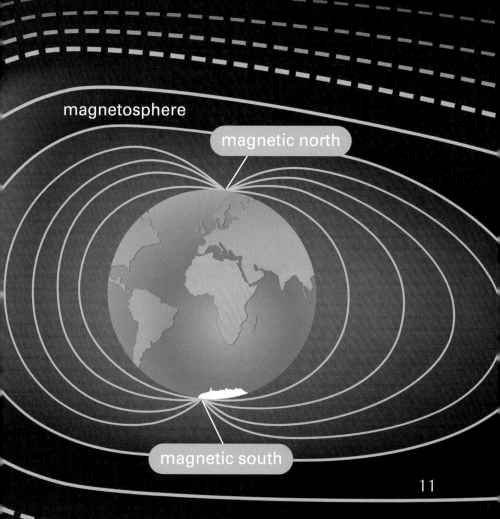

magnetosphere

magnetic north

magnetic south

The auroras, however, are strongest at certain times, and hardly visible at others. Why is this? It is all to do with the **solar cycle** and **sunspots**.

The Sun is made up of electrically-charged hot gas. This creates a magnetic field. Over a period of about 11 years (called the "solar cycle") intense patches of magnetic activity appear on the Sun's surface. When there are lots of these patches, auroras are at their strongest.

At the end of the 11 years, something strange happens: the north and south magnetic poles of the Sun (yes, the Sun has them too!) swap places. At this point, the cycle begins again. Eleven years later, the poles swap again – and so on and so on. It is in the middle of each cycle that there are the most sunspots and when auroras are most visible on Earth.

solar maximum
lots of sunspots
high chance of aurora

solar minimum
no sunspots
low chance of aurora

So, the solar cycle and the solar wind both have a part to play in what happens to create an aurora.

But it's the particular way in which the protons and electrons collide with gases in Earth's atmosphere which creates the shapes we see in the sky.

When the protons and electrons hit these gases, such as oxygen and nitrogen, they are pulled towards the magnetic north and south on Earth.

International Space Station

Then, because of the shape of Earth's magnetic field, the auroras form in ovals encircling the poles.

This image was taken from the International Space Station (ISS). The ISS is a craft that sits about 400 kilometres above Earth, and orbits it every 90 minutes. From the ISS, scientists from all over the world analyse space and conduct a range of experiments.

surface of Earth's southern hemisphere

auroral oval

Forms and shapes

Many people have tried to list the different forms of auroras. Scientists Stuart Clark and Asgeir Brekke came up with these categories.

Form	Description
a mild glow	Not very visible. They are seen near the horizon – but are easy to mix up with moonlit clouds.
patches	also look like clouds, but easier to see
arcs	like arches or bridges – they curve across the sky
rays	light or dark stripes which reach upwards
curtains	look as if they have folds or layers

curtains

Although the lights may appear to be shooting out of mountains, the closest they get to Earth is usually about 100 kilometres. This is about 300 times the height of the Eiffel Tower in Paris. A small number may make their way down to 80 kilometres. In part, it is these different distances from Earth that create the different colours you can see.

rays

patches

arcs above a glowing horizon

Different gases, different colours

Auroras can be many different colours. But why?

The reason is that there are lots of different gases in Earth's atmosphere, so the different colours come from the charged particles hitting different gases.

Firstly, Earth's atmosphere contains lots of oxygen. The typical colour created by oyxgen when it comes into contact with solar particles in the auroral oval is green. So, the most common forms of auroras tend to be green. Green is also the colour the eye is most sensitive to, so it's easier to spot.

However, when the oxygen is at a very high **altitude** and solar particles crash into it, it can produce a beautiful scarlet or crimson colour, rather than the more usual green light.

At lower altitudes, below 100 kilometres, oxygen is less common. Here, the nitrogen in the atmosphere can produce auroras which are blue. There is also nitrogen higher in the atmosphere, too, but the way oxygen interacts with it is different.

Other colours such as yellow have also been seen, although they are not as frequent. It all depends on the mix of gases and at what height they react with solar particles.

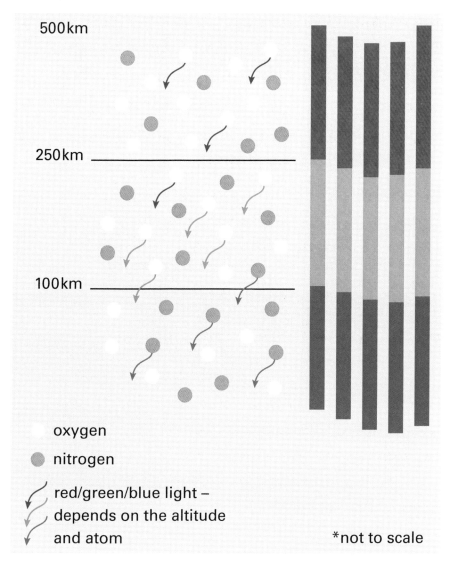

500km

250km

100km

oxygen
nitrogen
red/green/blue light –
depends on the altitude
and atom

*not to scale

The history of the auroras

It is possible that people noticed auroras thousands of years ago.

A Chinese tale from about 2600 BCE says:

Fu-Pao, the mother of the Yellow Empire Shuan-Yuan, saw strong lightning moving around the star Su, which belongs to the constellation of Beidou, and the light illuminated the whole area.

But how do we know she saw the auroras?

Well, "Beidou" is the Chinese term for the star pattern known as "the Plough" or "the Big Dipper".

The Plough

This pattern is located close to the Pole Star – which is positioned directly above the magnetic North Pole. And we know that that is a place you can typically see the auroras.

There is also an unusual painting which shows candles floating on top of clouds. Could this be a drawing of the lights?

early drawing of the aurora, depicted as candles in the sky, 1570

Seeing the lights for yourself

Seeing the lights is not easy. Lots of factors need to come together.

First, it must be dark!

You must avoid places with light **pollution**, such as cities. Light from buildings, cars and roads at nighttime can block out or make other lights in the sky difficult to see. The problem is that light from cars and buildings reflects back from the ground or other objects into the sky.

You also need a clear night without clouds.

Finally, you are more likely to see the auroras when the Sun is active. This doesn't mean you can see the Sun in the sky shaking or dancing! It doesn't refer to the Sun's visibility, either. If you remember, this means the time in the middle of the solar cycle when there are lots of sunspots.

Chasing the lights

The northern lights are visible from late August to early April during the hours of dark. In some parts of the northern hemisphere (such as parts of **Scandinavia**, Russia and Canada), it can be dark for 24 hours a day in winter.

Many people plan holidays to see the auroras. They seek out the best locations and travel to areas away from cities.

There is even a place called Aurora Village in Finland, where travellers can stay in glass igloos and watch the auroras from their beds. But even here, light pollution can affect the display. If this happens, some visitors use snow-sleds to travel further north.

Even then, the chance of catching a brilliant display is slim. Travellers are often advised to organise other activities to fill their time, for example, visiting glaciers or watching polar bears.

To see the southern lights, it is even more difficult. This is because there is far more ocean around the South Pole, and fewer landmasses where you can stay or watch them from.

However, the island of Tasmania off the coast of Australia is a good location. The best place of all is probably Antarctica, but it is a very difficult place to visit.

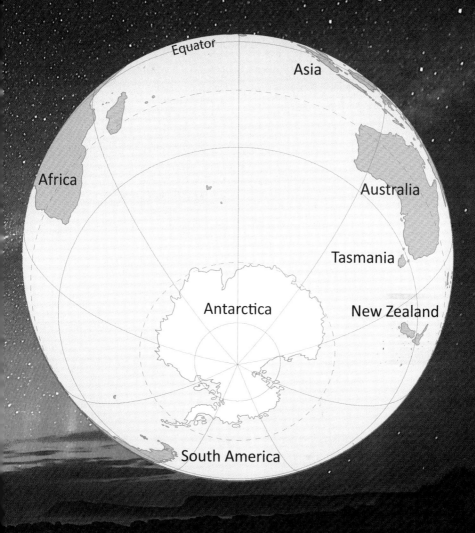

Equator

Asia

Africa

Australia

Tasmania

Antarctica

New Zealand

South America

Aurora hunters

For some people, seeing the auroras is more than just part of a holiday. They dedicate their whole life to seeing and photographing these lights. They belong to groups on social media and exchange news about when and where the next big display will happen.

They try to predict where the lights will appear using **meteorological data** (and charts on smartphone apps or websites).

Often, they sleep with a travel bag packed full of warm clothing so they can quickly go to a spot where the auroras might appear.

They can be compared with storm-chasers in places like the USA who try to predict where **tornadoes** will appear.

Myths and legends

Some people in the past often believed the appearance of the lights meant war was coming or that a sad event had taken place.

For example, some early Chinese legends suggest that the lights show a battle between good and evil dragons breathing fire. One **Norse** legend suggests the lights are reflections from the shields worn by the Valkyries, female servants to the gods.

The Inuits of Greenland imagined the lights were the souls of dead children playing in the sky.

Even as recently as the 18th and 19th century, some people linked the appearance of red auroras with revolution or war.

But not all legends link the lights to battles or sad events. Another Norse legend suggests that the auroras are the mythical Bifrost, a bridge in the form of a rainbow which links the gods to people on Earth.

"Valkyrien" (1869) by Norwegian painter Peter Nicolao Arbo showing a female warrior (Valkyrie) riding into battle

A fox made of fire

The Finnish word for the "aurora borealis" is "revontulet". This translates as "fox fires". But what has a fox got to do with the lights? There is a myth in Finland which says that the lights are caused by a fox whose tail causes bright sparks because he runs so rapidly across the **tundra**.

This probably sounds ridiculous, but there is a grain of scientific truth in the story. A fox's fur can be charged with static energy. This can create sparks when rubbed or when coming into contact with different materials or atmospheres. It is the same effect as when you rub a balloon against your jumper and then stick it on the wall or ceiling.

The Sami people, who live in the northern areas of Scandinavia and the Kola Peninsula, have a different word for the lights. They call them "guovssahasat" – a word connected to "guovssu", which means morning or evening glow. Many believe the lights are caused by the spume of water ejected by whales.

Fascinating art and stories

The auroras have fascinated lots of artists and writers.

One of the most famous paintings of the auroras is from 1865 by Frederic Edwin Church.

Can you see the tiny ship at the bottom? The painting was based on a real-life voyage by Arctic explorer, Isaac Israel Hayes. He brought back a sketch and also wrote about his experiences.

He mentioned the light was "chiefly red" but many different colours created a "fierce display". He described "countless tongues of white flame" which "rush aloft and lick the skies".

The powerful auroras

Sometimes fact is as strange as fiction.

On Friday 2nd September 1859, a particularly strong solar wind from the Sun hit Earth's magnetic field. It caused an aurora that was so bright the *New York Times* newspaper reported that it was: "so brilliant that at about one o'clock [at night] ordinary print could be read by the light."

Gold miners in the Rocky Mountains in the USA got up and started having breakfast because the glow was so bright they thought it was morning.

In those days, the quickest way to send messages was by using telegrams. Telegrams were simple messages created by tapping sounds into a machine – the equivalent of email today! The people who sent the messages – telegraph operators – had an even bigger surprise. Although power lines had been destroyed in the storm, they were still able to send messages using the electrical currents linked to the aurora. Some operators even got small electric shocks!

So, can the lights be dangerous too?

In fact, they don't pose a direct health risk for us here on Earth.

We are lucky to be protected by Earth's personal shield – the magnetosphere. But the electrically-charged particles *can* affect satellites and other technology. For example, communication between radio operators and pilots in aeroplanes could be affected. It is even possible that astronauts could get a huge dose of **radiation**, if there was a particularly powerful solar storm.

And that's not all. Because solar storms clash with Earth's magnetic field, certain animals and insects can be affected.

In 2016, 29 sperm whales were **beached** on North Sea coastlines. Scientists have suggested that the lights were to blame for their deaths. They believe that sperm whales might get their sense of direction from Earth's magnetic field. It is possible that a solar storm, similar to the ones that create the lights, could have affected the magnetosphere. This confused the whales and made them lose their way.

Birds, bees, bats and turtles – to name just a few – all get their sense of direction from the Earth's magnetic field. This means they know intuitively where north and south are.

Auroras on other planets

Earth is not the only planet where auroras can be seen. On other planets in our solar system, solar particles interact with each planet's atmosphere just like on Earth.

The particular colours of the lights depend on the gases on each planet.

Jupiter and Saturn have powerful **ultraviolet** and **infrared** auroras which look like loops or hoops. Unlike most of Earth's auroras, which hover close to Earth's surface, the auroras on Saturn can appear up to 1000 kilometres above the surface of the planet.

Unfortunately, these amazing auroras are not visible to the human eye and can only be seen through **telescopes** – but they make beautiful pictures!

For now, we will have to be content with the ones we *can* see, the lights that you might one day capture on your own camera.

Jupiter

Glossary

altitude height

beached when a whale swims on to a beach and can't get back into the water

electric charge a type of force felt by particles

electrons particles with a negative charge

hemisphere a half of a sphere (like half of a ball)

infrared a type of light not visible to human eyes

Latin an old language (no longer spoken) which forms the basis for French, Italian and several other languages

magnetic field area of magnetism created by poles, like Earth's North and South Poles

meteorological data facts and statistics about the weather

Norse belonging or relating to Scandinavian countries

particles very small parts of something

pollution something which harms or poisons the environment

protons particles with a positive charge

radiation energy created in the form of electromagnetic waves or as high-energy particles

Scandinavia region which covers Denmark, Norway, Sweden, Finland, Faroe Islands and Iceland

solar to do with the Sun

solar cycle a cycle of change in the Sun's magnetic activity which lasts about 11 years

sunspots spots of intense magnetic activity visible on the Sun's surface

telescopes instruments that use lenses to make distant objects look larger

tornadoes violent, spinning funnels of air caused by thunderstorms

tundra flat, frozen lands of the Arctic

ultraviolet a type of light not visible to human eyes

SEE THE
AMAZING
AURORAS

COME AND SEE THE
NORTHERN LIGHTS –
AURORA BOREALIS

From late August to early April

Join us in Norway, Finland, Iceland, Alaska or Siberia!

1. It must be dark (no light pollution)!

2. A clear night is best (no clouds, please).

3. The Sun needs to be active.

Visit glaciers or watch polar bears while you wait!

COME AND SEE THE SOUTHERN LIGHTS – AURORA AUSTRALIS

From late August to early April

Join us on the island of Tasmania, off the coast of Australia – or in Antarctica!

Don't miss this incredible natural wonder!!

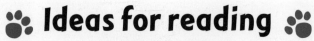

🐾 Ideas for reading 🐾

Written by Gill Matthews
Primary Literacy Consultant

Reading objectives:

- ask questions to improve their understanding of a text
- identify main ideas drawn from more than one paragraph and summarising these
- retrieve, record and present information from non-fiction

Spoken language objectives:

- articulate and justify answers, arguments and opinions
- maintain attention and participate actively in collaborative conversations, staying on topic and initiating and responding to comments
- ask relevant questions to extend their understanding and knowledge

Curriculum links: Science – States of matter; Geography – Locational knowledge

Interest words: fierce, countless, aloft

Resources: ICT; Art materials

Build a context for reading

- Ask children to look at the front cover and read the title. Check their understanding of auroras. Read the back cover blurb. Ask them to describe the auroras shown on the cover and how they feel about them.
- Discuss what sort of book children think this is and what features they expect to find in it. Encourage them to develop questions that they think will be answered in the book.
- Ask children to find the contents page. Ask which section they think would give information about what auroras are.
- Read pp2–7. Ask children to summarise what auroras are.

Understand and apply reading strategies

- Return to the contents page. Explain that you want to find out what makes auroras happen. Ask children to suggest which section will give that information.